A
TREASURE
OF LIFESAVERS FOR
VICTORIOUS LIVING

GERALDINE MORGAN

ISBN 978-1-0980-3157-2 (paperback)
ISBN 978-1-0980-3158-9 (digital)

Christian Faith Publishing, Inc.
832 Park Avenue
Meadville, PA 16335
www.christianfaithpublishing.com

All scriptures are quoted from the King James Version unless otherwise noted.

Printed in the United States of America

Dedication

This book has been a long time coming!
I give God all the honor and glory, for
without Him, I can do nothing.
It is with great joy, yet sadness, that I dedicate my first book, *A Treasure of Lifesavers for Victorious Living*, to my dad, the late Apostle John H. Boyd, Sr. He was my friend, my pastor, and my hero. It was because of the foundation he gave to me that I can pursue the purpose and destiny God had designed for my life.
When the enemy thought he had the upper hand, I remembered the golden nuggets my dad gave me.
My dad would say to me,

"Feed your faith and starve your doubts!
Read the Word and do what it says!
Speak life and make things happen!
God can do more for you in five minutes,
then you can do for yourself in a lifetime."

Thank you, Dad, for all of your golden nuggets.
I will forever hold them in my heart.

CONTENTS

FOREWORD

I am so excited about what God is doing in the life of my wife, Geraldine. I thank God every day for this diamond that has been placed in my life. I salute her as she continues to write and ignite the fire in women from all walks of life.

A Treasure of Lifesavers for Victorious Living is a collaboration of powerful declarations, words of wisdom, and nuggets with a foundation established on The Word of God. These writings affirm that life and death are in the power of the tongue. Any of these poems and affirmations can be read daily. They are intended to empower women to defeat and conquer fear, doubt, and obstacles that are encountered in life.

Geraldine is in pursuit of reaching women who are hurt, abused, confused and in despair. Her desire is to renew their minds and thoughts by speaking what God has spoken in His Word for their lives. She understands that the declaration of The Word of God will bring forth the manifestation of God's power. She has set forth this book to speak to every woman. This book has inspirations and devotionals that will stimulate and motivate you in your daily walk with God.

Since the enemy is an expert at attacking the mind, it is imperative for you to decree and declare The Word of God over your life every day. Allow this book of lifesavers to propel you into the purpose God has created you for. After reading these declarations, you will no longer identify as a victim, instead you will proclaim victory!

This is your time! Read this book and live victoriously!

Dr. Caswell Morgan
Dean of the New Greater Bethel Bible Institute
Advisory Board of Eldership of New Greater Bethel Ministries
Queens, New York

ACKNOWLEDGMENTS

*F*irst and foremost, thank You, Lord, for Your unconditional love, mercy, and grace. You are my king and the very air that I breathe. I could never find the words or give enough praises to express my love and desire for You.

To my husband and best friend, Caswell Morgan, you are the one that holds the key to my heart. Together, we have built a solid relationship where love flows, a home where we feel safe, and a family filled with love. Thank you for sharing my life, being my love, and helping make my dreams come true. You have encouraged me and inspired me to be all that God has destined for me to become. God created you just for me. My love for you will always be in my heart.

To my four children—Lora, Lance, Toby, and Dabari—you all are my joy and inspiration. You each have been there for me through thick and thin and my ups and downs. You are priceless and untradeable! I say thank you. You are all my cheerleaders.

To all of my grands and great-grands, you have Gigi's heart always.

To my sisters, Gail, Rubina, and Desiray; to my brothers, John and Warren, thank you for all the support and prayers you all have sent my way.

To my spiritual family, the New Greater Bethel Ministries (NGBM); Pastor John H. Boyd II; Lady Valerie Boyd; Prophetess Dr. Juanita Bynum; and Pastor Andre Jones and Co-Pastor Rachel Jones of Ruach City Church, thank you all for your love and encouragement.

Finally, to all my extended family and friends whom I love and appreciate, I say thank you.

CHAPTER 1

Morning Starters

*I*n this chapter of "Morning Starters," these poems and declarations are read at the start of your day. They are meant to spark your day and inspire you to pursue God's plan for your life!

As morning starters, they can be read during morning prayer. And if you are able, it is suggested that you memorized these morning starters to recite while driving, riding the train or bus to work.

As breakfast is the most important meal of the day, so are the morning thoughts that inspire you for your day. These morning starters will strengthen you for the challenges ahead and keep you motivated to conquer the things ahead.

Don't start your morning without your morning starters.

Yes, You Can

Geraldine Morgan

*I*f a flower can grow through the cracks of the concrete,
If a caterpillar can become a butterfly,
And if the doomed bumblebee, which was never supposed to fly,
defies the odds to fly,
I must ask you: Why can't you?

You can grow through the cracks of heartbreak.
You can transform into a butterfly like a caterpillar.
You were doomed never to reach the sky,
But I know you can fly.

Yes, you can!

STARTING MY MORNING WITH YOU
Geraldine Morgan

*I*t's the dawning of a new day!
As my feet hit the floor,
Prayer and praise—it's how I start the day with You.

With uplifted hands,
With my voice, I began to shout,
This is the day that the Lord has made,
I will rejoice and be glad in it!

Lord, I acknowledge You.
Direct my path,
Let my footsteps be ordered by You.
I must not simply serve You but please You.
I must do all I need to do to make my day an accomplishment.
I will put You first other than myself.

Today is a day of Your favor in my life.
I will speak words that are seasoned with grace.
I am above and not beneath.
I am the head and not the tail.
I will loan and not borrow.
Everything I put my hands to do will be blessed.
Favor is going to do what money can't.
For I am blessed!

I start my day with You.
Therefore, You will be with me this day.

OPPORTUNITY
Debra Charles

*W*aiting…
Waiting for doors to open for me!
Waiting…
Expecting someone to see what I see!
Waiting…
A day goes by, two, and then three.
Waiting…
When is God going to prepare the way for me?
My dream, yes, that dream…
Waiting…

Waiting…
I'm waiting for the right opportunity,
Opportunity for expansion,
Opportunity to be, to do, and to have,
Opportunity for creating…

Today, I will open my eyes to the endless opportunities that surround
    me.
Today, I will see each moment as a new opportunity to express my
    potential.
Misused, abused. and confused, this is not me.
Depressed, bewildered, overwhelmed, this is not me.
This is not me… No, this is not me.
I am no longer waiting for opportunity.
Opportunity meets me daily.

My God has afforded me opportunity,
And with every opportunity
Comes new prospects, new possibilities, new advantages, and new
      interests.

So when opportunities appear,
I will move quickly and confidently!
When opportunity knocks,
I will open the door,
I will pursue,
I…will…act!
I am no longer waiting.

A Better Morning
Geraldine Morgan

I have changed my morning starter to a better brand.
I no longer drink Sanka or Folgers or any other coffee.
They're tasteless and bland to my soul.

At times, I cannot reach the altar of prayer.
However, I still have my Comforter, my Defender, and my Mind
    Regulator.

He has been moved from the back burner of my life
And became my number one source of morning fire.
He has changed this sinner—this viler
Into a brand-new, soul-winning creature!

Great is He that lives in me.
No longer am I a quitter, a failure, a mourner
For I was created, molded, sculpted, chiseled, and cleansed by my
    Master!

I will be, now and forever, a conqueror and a leader,
Someone with a future,
Someone with visions and dreams,
And above all,
Someone who is like an eagle
Soaring in pursuit of destiny!

My morning is better because I have You.

Morning Champion
Chanel Ramsay

I am a champion.
Therefore, I am victorious in every situation life may bring to me.
I am a giver.
Therefore, I expect a great harvest.
I am anointed.
Therefore, I can handle this.
I am an overcomer.
Therefore, I will overcome evil with good.
I am a praiser.
Therefore, I will dance as David danced.

I am living the life of a conqueror.
I am blessed to be a planter.
God's favor rests on every sower in my life.

I am a believer in everything God has promised me.
My expectation shall not be disappointed.
My life is full of vision, purpose, wisdom, joy, and strength.

By the power and authority invested in me,
I boldly confess: it's raining increase and abundance in my life.
Lord, my hope rests only in You in Jesus's name.

HALLELUJAH
Monette Berry

*H*allelujah,
I am more than a conqueror.
Hallelujah,
I am victorious, blessed, and an anointed believer of Christ.
Hallelujah,
I have a purpose, wisdom, favor, and hope.
Hallelujah,
He has become my joy, strength, and abundance.
Hallelujah,
My expectations will turn into blessings because of His power and authority.
Hallelujah, hallelujah, hallelujah!

I WILL

Geraldine Morgan

I am a child of the living God.
I am the heir and a joint heir with Christ.
I have the righteousness of God and the mind of Christ.
I will see the invisible; I will do the impossible.
I will touch the intangible; I will achieve the incredible.
I am God's idea, and God cannot fail.
Therefore, I can do all things through Christ, which strengthens me.

I will not struggle to be recognized, for my gift shall announce me.
I will take charge of my life as I master my time.
I will grow in wisdom and in stature.
I will walk in dominion over every situation.
I will walk in divine health; no sickness or disease shall abide in this
    body.
I am blessed beyond curses, raised above terror and established
    beyond oppression.

I will do the right thing at the right time.
I shall fulfill and not frustrate my destiny.
I will have prosperity.
I will live an abundant life.
No weapon formed against me shall prosper.
I am an overcomer.
The Greater One lives in me!

CHAPTER 2

Afternoon Inspirations

*A*s the day progresses and the challenges ahead become clear, the enemy finds his way to move into your mind. His intent, as always, is to kill, steal, and destroy you at all costs.

Therefore, read and meditate on "Afternoon Inspirations."

"Afternoon Inspirations" are quick jumpstarts to bring you back to the Word of God and His love for you. Read "Afternoon Inspirations" when you're discouraged and in despair. Read them when you're having a grand day or a bad day. Read them even when you don't feel like it. Read them to remain focused and unwavering.

Allow "Afternoon Inspirations" to rejuvenate your mind and soul.

I Was and Still Am
Geraldine Morgan

I began to think back on who I was and what I have become.
I was someone with goals, gifts, and vision.
I was full of talent and wisdom.
I was focused on ideas, achievements, and other aspirations.
I was…

Yet I remember,
I still am…
I am still someone.
I am one of God's creations.
I have dominion and power!
It is He that has given me that authority.
I have the keys in my hand.

I continue to stand proud, tall, and face the day's fears bravely.
I am a rare gem—a ruby, if you please.
I sparkle. I am worthy. I am a precious stone of wonders.

God has been searching endlessly for those to help complete His
    mission.
I filled out an application, and guess what?
I was assigned a mission from Him.

I am the future generation.
I shall tread upon the nations.
There are no limitations.
I am not labeled as "many are called," for I am chosen as one of God's
      secret weapons.
And I still am…

HALF OF THE DAY IS DONE
Var Kelly

O my Lord!
Half of the day is done!
I still have so much to be done!
This project, this phone call, this meeting.
They all need to be done!

O Lord!
What's this?
An issue? A problem? A challenge?
Why is that lost?
Who did it?
Who can fix it?

Yes, Lord!
I feel You near.
Yes, Lord!
Your peace is here.
Yes, Lord!
I know what to do.
Thank You, Lord!
You always come through.

O my Lord!
Half of the day is done!
Oh, the joy I have;
Oh, the renewed strength I have;
You always put me in the right place.

O my Lord!
Half of the day is done!
Oh, what I will do in Your name.
Oh, what You will work through me.
Oh, how you will demonstrate Your Power.

O my Lord!
Half of the day is done!
You will work through me.
You have strengthened me.
I will be a conqueror again.

O my Lord!
Half of the day is done!
I'm excited again.
All things are possible.
There's no problem.
I can fix it.
That project—done.
That phone call—done.
That meeting—done.
Praise the Lord!
Half of the day is done!

MIDDAY REMINDER
Geraldine Morgan

I look at myself in the mirror to see.
I laugh…
I smile…
I live…
Beauty is inside me!

You too,
You are as beautiful as you want to be.
Look…
See…
Shine your light.

You smile,
You live,
You do,
You dream,
You accomplish.

Be as blessed as can be!
Be as sharp as the letter *t*!
Stand, look, and stare like me!

Say these words with me:
I will allow myself to dream.
I will move like the water in a stream.
I will fly like the dove in the sky above!
I will even do more than a conqueror; yes, they will see.

I am excited!
It's time to give.
I've got to live.
Can't shrug my shoulders.
I must continue to dig.

My mind is now renewed!
I think big!
Champion, winner, victorious!
Overcomer, believer, conqueror, and blessed!
All of that is me.

I Am Not an Accident
Fabian Stevens

*I*t was the Lord who made the earth and created mankind for it. His own hands stretched out the heavens and created the earth to yield in its season. It is His by design. I live and move in it—in His creation.

I am here for a purpose. I am created for a purpose. My mission is to become a servant for the Lord. I am what I am, for He has made me. I am designed solely for Christ. I am alive because God wanted me to be created. The Bible says, "The Lord will fulfill His purpose for me."

Regardless of how others may see it, the Lord is transforming me in many areas of my life. Piece by piece, layer upon layer, the inner and outer core—plastering, chiseling, carving, and reshaping—He is transforming me until I am sculpted into His image.

He knew since the beginning of time; He knew the precise time that He would breathe life into me. It was not by chance; "no if, and, or but" about it. It was all about His purpose and His plan.

I am not a mistake. It was predestined. I am the DNA that God has created—His most valuable creation.

Scientists have proven the earth was made for mankind. God formed the earth. He did not create it to be empty but formed it to be inhabited. Why? For the simple fact of love. He did it out of love. He is love.

God created me; He has given me life abundantly. Therefore, I was no accident. God makes no mistakes. I am no accident. Step by step, I am custom made. Step by step, I am tailored made. Step by step, I am God's plan. I am His divine plan. I have a divine purpose. I am restricted to some but wholly exclusive for Him, selected by Him, and one of His elite.

I have asked God: Why me? Each time I ask, He lifts me up; He never tears me down. I go through trials, but through Him, I am made stronger. I am wonderfully and fearfully made. No one has the right or privilege to take that away. I am no mistake. I am no human error. I am God's beloved—an exclusive package, a brand made by God. I bear the Master's seal. It cannot be broken. His mark is on me. I am not an accident.

Your Promise from God
Geraldine Morgan

*Y*our promise has a purpose, and
You are the recipient.

Obedience is an attachment.
It causes manifestation to erupt.

Never let expectation take a rest.
Your inheritance can't be denied.

In your due seasons of release and
Despite the challenges and tests,
You will reap.

Who Is Inside of You?
Geraldine Morgan

I s there a little girl inside of you?
A little girl that just won't grow up?
Does she cry?
Throw tantrums?
Fail spiritual tests?

She envies her sisters—
The one's who moved ahead.
It frustrates her.
Makes her feel she's at a standstill.

Pain seems to dominate her actions.
Past hurts, unforgiveness, abuse, and secrets;
They all weigh her down.

Little girl!
Little girl!
It's time to grow up!
You've been stuck in the spider's web long enough.

Little girl!
Little girl!
You can't get to your future
While holding on to your past.

Little girl!
Little girl!
It's time to move ahead.
Open your heart, your eyes, and your ears.
Hear what God is saying to you.

Little girl!
Little girl!
It's time to put her to rest.
Inside of you is a virtuous woman—
God's virtuous woman!

NEXT
Geraldine Morgan

*L*ife on earth is just a dress rehearsal,
A rehearsal before the real production.
Earth is the staging area,
The area before the actual production execution.

Life is the practice workout
Before the actual game.
It's the warm up
Before the actual race.

While life on earth offers many choices,
Eternity offers only two:
Heaven or hell.
This life is preparation for the next.

When measured against eternity,
Our time on earth is a blink of an eye,
But the consequences of it will last forever.

Live each day as if it were the last day of your life.
There is more to life than just here and now.
There is a next.
Choose what you do today wisely.

THIS DAY
Var Kelly

*T*his day has made me quit.
This day has brought on fear.
I started out with joy and gladness
But was met with the devil's weapons of destruction.

This day made me lose hope.
This day made me wonder if I should continue.
What seemed like a little thing
Has turned into this big thing.

The enemy desires to shift me out.
He desires to make me doubt my purpose.
He desires to steal my joy and gladness—my hope.

Yet, I recall this is God's day.
He made it.
I still rejoice in it.

So for the rest of this day,
I allow my Father's power to enthrall me.
I allow His love to fill me.
His cross reminds me of love.
And I am no longer afraid of this day.

I move forward to beat every battle,
Conquer every devil,
Jump over every trap,
And defeat every challenge.
For this day started joyful with Him,
And I will end with joy in Him this day.

PURPOSE AND DESTINY
Geraldine Morgan

God created purpose and destiny.
When you were born, He made you part of His purpose and destiny.
Only in God can you discover your purpose and destiny.

In order to know your purpose in life,
You must know God's Word
And live the Word,
Then know not the wisdom of this world.

God was thinking of you,
Thinking of you long before you thought of Him.
He planned your purpose before you existed.

The Lord will fulfil His purpose through you.
Unplanned by your parents but planned by God.
God never does anything accidentally.
He has a reason for everything.

Knowing your purpose gives meaning to your life.
Without God, your life has no purpose.
Without purpose, your life has no meaning.
And without meaning, your life has no hope.

Without a clear purpose,
You will keep changing directions;
New jobs, new relationships,
Hoping the change will settle confusion
Or bring fulfillment.

Knowing your purpose motivates your life.
It produces passion.
It energizes life.
It clears the path.

Know your purpose.
Fulfill your destiny.

CHAPTER 3

Evening Meditations

The day is almost over, and plans that were initiated may not have been completed. At the same time, goals may have been accomplished and finished with vigor and power.

"Evening Meditations" are meant to allow your mind to ease into the evening as you prepare to rest and sleep.

Read "Evening Meditations" and allow yourself to be spiritually put at ease by the poetic flow and evening aspirations outlined in this chapter. Allow yourself to again see the vision that God gave you.

Make ready to receive new strength as you prepare to rest from the day's toil and trouble.

TIMEOUT
Geraldine Morgan

*F*rom the hustle and bustle of my busy day;
Rising early in the morning,
And no break in between.
I need... I need...
I need a timeout.

Timeout...
I need a breath of fresh air.
Timeout...
I need time to calm me.
Timeout...
I need to break up this fallow ground.
Timeout...
I need time to appreciate me.
Timeout...
I need time to meditate and pray.
Timeout...
I need time to refresh before the new sun begins.

I need to set aside time.
Time anywhere in a small corner.
Maybe time in the back seat of my car,
Under a tree,
Or a stroll on the streets.
I need a timeout.
Lord, I need a timeout!

LORD, CAN WE TALK?
Var Kelly

*T*he day has taken all my strength.
I don't think I have anything left to give.
The sun is dimming,
But the day hasn't fully ended.
I still need to do this and that,
But I don't have strength.

There's still dinner to cook,
Clothes to wash, a conference phone call,
And several other things.
I don't have the strength.

Lord, can we talk?
I come to you this time of the day.
You are my help.
You always give me what I need.
You load me with grace and mercy daily.
You are divine in power and strength.
So I come to you.

Restore me.
Empower me.
Help me to do what I need to do.
Help me to prioritize and focus.
I need divine strength.
I need to serve my family, my church, and You.
Give me more strength.

I hear You.
Go this way,
Don't do that,
Do it this way,
That can wait until tomorrow.

You instruct me,
You direct me.
My path is made clear.

I had no strength,
But I talked to You,
And You strengthened me.
Thank God for the talk.
Thank God for His strength.

THROUGH SONGS OF PRAISE
Geraldine Morgan

*H*e's all I need (1)

I love Jesus.
He's been so good to me.
I love Jesus.
He died on Calvary.
I love Jesus.
I take Him wherever I go.
I love Jesus.
He is the lover of my soul.

He's all I need.
He's all I need.
Jesus is all I need.

The storm may rise,
The winds may blow,
But this one thing I know…

He's all I need.
He's all I need.
Jesus is all I need.

Wonderful Jesus (2)

Wonderful Jesus,
Wonderful Lord,
You are my sunshine,
You are my joy.

I praise your name,
From morning 'til night.
His praises shall continuously be in my mouth.

Wonderful Jesus,
Wonderful Lord,
You are the joy and strength of my life.

SWEET SLEEP
Var Kelly

*Y*es, Lord!
These blankets are warm.
Yes, Lord!
These pillows are fluffy.
Yes, Lord!
I need this sleep.

Thank You, Lord,
I have a place to rest my body.
A place to call home.
A place to be protected from the elements.
A place where my family lives and rest.

As I lay me down to sleep,
I know my sleep will be sweet.
My soul You keep.
My body You restore.
My mind is at peace.

As I lay me down to sleep,
There are no bitter dreams,
No tossing and turning.
There is sweet sleep.

Thank You, Lord!
I feel you rocking me to sleep.
I take in your perfect peace.
Now I go to sleep.

I Lift Up Holy Hands
Geraldine Morgan

*Y*ou are my Lord,
You are my King.
I lift up holy hands to Thee.

For the mercy and grace that was given me,
For the favor that has been released to me,
For your Word that guide me day by day,
For all that you do,
I lift up holy hands to Thee.

Angelical Prayer
Geraldine Morgan

*J*esus, I thank You for divine rest.
As you download the Word during my sleep,
Give unto me instructions,
Warning, corrections, and comfort.
Let healing and deliverance be released over me.

Jesus, I thank You for release.
Let my thought patterns be enlighten,
Show me visions and dreams
That produce much fruit.

Jesus, I thank You for protection.
You cancel out negativity,
Remove distractions and hindrances.
Your blood prevails.

Jesus, I thank You for my mind.
I think on things that are honest;
I think on things that are lovely
And things that are true;
I sleep and rest in You.

Amen.

CHAPTER 4

Midnight Cry

*T*here are times when sleep won't come. We close our eyes and meditate on the goodness of God, yet trouble and warfare meet us. It causes us not to rest. Other times, our sleep may be disturbed and troubled by dreams and constant visuals of defeat.

During these times of the night, we sometimes need to have our minds redirected to God's awesome power and love through prayer and supplication.

"Midnight Cry" is a chapter meant to be read during troubling times of the night. The flow of this chapter varies by the type of cries that can occur during the night.

THERE IS ALWAYS WORSE
Geraldine Morgan

*P*ity, rage, anger—that's what you feel inside!
You say to yourself, "Life has treated me unfairly."
You ask, "Where are You, God?"
You cry out, asking God, "Why me?"

Abused, raped, molested,
Yet you survived with a clean bill of health.
Others you knew experienced all the above and worse.
Many contracted AIDS, and some succumbed to an early grave.

Betrayed, unfaithful, he divorced you.
The man who said he loved you.
He played you.

Yet you're restored.
You have a new Man in your life.
He who carved you in the palm of His hands,
He who created you to become a statue of beauty,
He is your new Man.

Yet there is worse.
You remember the others.
It brings you much pain.
The others who never had a chance to meet the Man;
The Man who brought you out.
They allowed the suicide demon to take away their life.

Yet there is worse.
What about those who are homeless and need to eat?
An offer came from the streets they could not refuse.
It landed them in jail—a place of no return.

So before you quit, give up, or throw in the towel,
Visit the hospitals, walk through the jails,
Look at the homeless, the mental institutions too,
And finally, don't forget to put the cemetery on that list too.
And then you will see the challenges, circumstances, and the state of
     mind you could have been.
There is always worse.

Through poverty, unemployment, and sickness,
You made it through.
Don't forget the others that's worse off than you.
Minister to them.
Remember them.
Pray for them.

It could be worse for them and for you.
There's always worse,
But if not for the grace of God,
It would be worse.

PAIN—THIS, TOO, SHALL PASS
Geraldine Morgan

*Y*ou say to yourself, "This pain, when will it end?"
You ask, "Was I purposed to live like this?
To be abused, tortured, and condemned?"
You say, "I think *not.*"

You are the apple of someone's eye.
In this world, there's someone who loves you.
They want to take this pain away.
In your heart, you know that "this too shall pass."

As you walk to find the person to take away the pain,
You will discover that the journey is not that far.
You will find that His hug will fill you with love, and you will know
    that this love is from above.

The shame and the pain from all your previous lashes
Will turn to ashes like burned pages.
He will turn your current frown upside down.
His smile will be so gorgeous, just like a freshly covered snow blanket
    on the ground.

This pain—this too shall pass!
Your joy will come in the morning.
No more crying, and no more mourning
Because you remember "this too shall pass."

DEPRESSION
Emma Watson

D is for *down* in the pits I go.

E is for the *everlasting* hurt and pain I endure.

P is for the *persistent* memories of my past in my heart and mind.

R is for the *recurring* voices that I hear rambling around in my head.

E is for the *eerie* thought that I would be better off dead.

S is for the *solace* that I so eagerly seek.

S is for the *sense* of reality that keeps me in bed.

I is for the *inspiration* of hope that gives me a peace of mind.

O is for the *open* call that Jesus saves and can set me free.

N is for *never again will I allow depression to take over me*!

You Cannot Hold Me
Chanel Ramsay

*T*hough you fill my mind
With constant fears,
Depression, you cannot hold me.

Though you flood my face
With regretful tears,
Depression, you cannot hold me.

Because I understand who I am
And why I am here,
Depression, you cannot hold me.

You tempt me and try me
To see if your grip will hold.
You sit and wait for me,
Hoping my faith will fold.
But you, depression,
Depression, you cannot hold me.

Stop, look, and listen.
Depression,
You are already a defeated foe.
You live no longer with me.
You no longer trouble my mind.

You no longer have residence.
Depression, you cannot hold me.
Depart from me.
I know you no more.

THE NIGHT TO THE MORNING
Geraldine Morgan

*Y*ou are greater than your past. You are stronger than any moment of failure. You can rise like smoke up a chimney. You were meant to spiral to the sky. All of the broken promises should not deny you the gift of life. Never forget that you are alive—sometimes weak, sometimes strong, but alive. You will be right some days and wrong some nights, but don't stop waking up in the morning. The morning is God's gift of another chance to pass the exam.

He has loved you gently, tenderly, and definitely. He has loved you with the gentle love of the Father's favor whose tenderness would shield you from the traumas of the past. You have been touched, blessed, and loved; you have been loved by the Father Himself. No wonder Satan has failed to destroy you in the night, for God has prepared you to be a light!

This truth is what you have to know if you are to withstand the darkness. This truth is what you must rehearse against the goblins of old images and past memories that would assault your dreams and turn them into nightmares. No matter how foreign this place in your life may seem, you must know He prepared you for it. He shielded you, and you are safe and secure. You may rest in the safety of His arms that will not fail you.

The morning is for the hopeful, not the regretful. It is an expectation. It is the wet dew moistening the dry ground. It is the hummingbirds and honking horns and a city yawning into alertness. Greater still, it is the future lying naked before you. Daybreak is stretching in the hours of a new opportunity just created. It is a filled manger and an empty tomb. It is life, love, and hope. Never forget about the breaking of day. It will come.

The night will pass, tears will dry, and enemies will leave; but you will arise in the morning!

FREE ME FROM UNFORGIVENESS
Patsy Rizzo

I wandered in sorrow and pain.
I did not know I had so many chains.
Like a caged bird who never sings,
I could not hear my heart ring.
The darkness overshadowed the light.
I asked God, "Will everything be alright?"
He said, "Little girl, I am here.
If you release it to me, I will draw you near."
So I released the bitterness, hurt, and pain.
I forgave all those I blamed,
Opened my heart, and flew free.

I am forgiven.
I forgive them.
He forgives me.
Thank God,
Now I am truly free.

DEPRESSION CRY
Patsy Rizzo

*M*y soul is cast down
In a pit where only darkness is seen.
In this pit, it's dark and cold.

How do I fill my wounded soul?
My heart beats, but I rarely hear it.
Is there anyone who really cares?
It seems like everyone is always better than me.

O God! How can this be?
You are the Master who created me.
You said, "My child, can you not see that you belong to Me?
So out of the pit, I must go.
I let the light of God show.
"Goodbye, pit" is what I state.
"So long, pain" is what I declare.

The Master has called me to a greater gain.
I have no time for depression.
I have no more darkness.
That pit is long gone.
I am past it.
I am over it.
Now I continue on.

It's Never Too Late
Geraldine Morgan

*L*ift up your head.
Don't write yourself off.
Why did you stop living?
Don't let all your dreams be put on hold.

What happened to the gifts?
God graced you with them.
Use them to allow others to live.

Let the past go.
Let self-pity go.
Let the passion arise.
Wake up the inner you.
Start with what you have *now*.

Time is of the essence.
All you need to say is yes.
Get up, and start moving.
It's the dawn of your new day.
Smile and laugh; go make it happen.
And always remember this:
It's never too late.

CHAPTER 5

Potpourri

*A*s potpourri is a mixture of dried flowers and petals mixed together, so are poems of this chapter. This chapter contains a mixture of poems meant to be read as often as needed. They vary in type and purpose, but they all come together to make a sweet smell.

As you read this chapter, read them with care and love. Read them day or night and especially when things just *ain't* right.

I Am a Designer's Original

Geraldine Morgan

I am clothed.
A designer's original.
Created inside and out,
In my mother's womb.

I am beautiful.
A designer's original.
Made with care.
Made with love.

I am a worshipper.
I worship only You.
With my heart, soul, and body,
To Thee I give You—me.

I am cute.
A designer's original.
Every hair on my head, fake or true,
You know them all,
You know the truth.

I am alive.
A designer's original.
You birthed me and watched me grow.
Now I live.
For I am fearfully and wonderfully made.

The Power of the Tongue

Geraldine Morgan

*E*xpectations that birth vision!
Hope that ignites purpose!
Wisdom that demands increase!
I speak it!

Abundance that brings joy!
Strength that produces power!
Authority that commands favor!
I speak it!

I am somebody!
I am an appointed seed!
I will keep my appointment with destiny!

I let go!
God has loosed me!
No more chains are hindering me!

I speak life!
I celebrate my deliverance!
I celebrate my victory!

I have authority!
I have dominion!
He gave it to me!

My tongue speaks!
My lips move!
I speak life and not death!

I have the power!
The power is in my tongue!
I speak life not only for me
But for each and every one!

There's a Worshipper in You

Geraldine Morgan

As you fall and bow down to pray,
The tears start to stream.
Your heart begins to release, and
The worshipper appears.

As you began to pour out your soul,
A flow of God's love streams in.
Cries of gratitude begin.
His grace and mercy have done it again.

Oh, the adoration.
Oh, the sweet smell.
As you bask in His presence,
He begins to pour in.

Let the consuming fire consume you.
Let the worship begin.
There's a worshipper in you.
Let Him come in.

SFGTD Box
Geraldine Morgan

*I*f life happens to deliver a situation to you that you cannot handle, do not attempt to resolve it yourself. Kindly put it in the "Something for God to Do (SFGTD)" box. He will get to it in time. All situations will be resolved not in your time but in God's time.

Once the matter is placed into the box, leave it there. Do not pick it up. Do not try to retrieve it. Leave it there. Go on with your day. Focus on His blessings, and leave the box with Him.

What It Means to Be Free

Geraldine Morgan

*W*hat does it mean to be free?
There's no worry, no fear, and no anxiety.
And surely, there's no depression.
They're all out the door.

What does it mean to be free?
There's no thought for tomorrow.
You remember you're a child of the King.
All burdens are lifted.
There's no heavy heart.
All shackles are loose.

What does it mean to be free?
What people say has no effect on you.
Their tongue of bondage no longer offends you.
Those curses no longer hinder you.
You barely remember them.
And now you laugh at them.

God has set you free.
His peace compasses all things.
His understanding resides in you.
You've searched for freedom.
You search no more.
You have a relationship with the King.
You are truly free.

LIVING WATER
Geraldine Morgan

*A*re you drinking from a fountain that never runs dry?
Are you drinking from living water that only the Master can supply?

It's life-changing for any circumstance you face.
It's not from a well, river, ocean, or lake.
It's from the Master,
He's the living water you must drink.

It bought new life to a woman at a well.
It will bring new life to you as well.

Are you thirsty?
Do you want to drink?
Take it all in, and take as much as you need.

If you keep drinking,
There will be a flow out of your belly.
Out of you will come blessings and not curses,
Glory and not condemnation,
Love and not destruction.

Yes, living water,
That's what you need to drink.
Come to Him.
Come take a drink.

PRAYER FOR INCREASE
Unknown

*H*eavenly Father, most gracious and loving God, I pray that You abundantly bless me.

I thank You, Lord, for the blessings I have received and for the blessings yet to come.

Dear God, I send up a prayer request for financial blessings, and not for me only, but for all who reads this prayer.

The power of joint prayer by those who believe and trust in You is more powerful than anything. So I and the reader join together to pray for the increase. We both thank You in advance for Your blessings.

Dear God, if the reader has a debt problem, deliver them from the burdens. Release your godly wisdom that they may be a good steward over all that You have given them.

God, I know how wonderful and mighty you are. So we commit to obey and walk in Your Word by faith the size of a mustard seed—that's all it takes.

We believe and ask all of this in Jesus name. Amen.

DECREE AND DECLARE
Geraldine Morgan

I decree and declare,
I have supernatural strength and the ability to fight the good fight
of truth!

I decree and declare,
I am a shareholder of God's inheritance. My family is rooted and
established in the faith.

I decree and declare,
I am a steward of great wealth, an ambassador for Christ, and the
Light of the World.

I decree and declare,
God has put a hedge of protection around me, endowed me with
wisdom, knowledge, and understanding.

I decree and declare,
I have the authority and power to expose the tactics of Satan.

I decree and declare,
That God has announced blessings and favor over my life.

I decree and declare,
For it is not by power nor by might, but by His Spirit, saith the Lord!

I am a
Champion
Winner
Giver
Overcomer
Praiser
Believer
Sower
Planter
Conqueror
Victor
Blessing
Anointed

I have
Expectations
Hope
Increase
Abundance
Power
Authority
Vision
Purpose
Wisdom
Joy
Strength
Favor

I decree and declare,
I am an heir to a heavenly inheritance.
It will manifest here on earth and be complete in heaven.

Glory hallelujah!
Praise the Lord!
I am what I am!
I have spoken it!

I WRITE
Geraldine Morgan

As a deer pantheth after the waters so my soul seeketh after God.
—Psalms 42:1

*W*ith passion within me, I write with my pen,
My thoughts from a day's journey.
I can express from my heart,
I can share with my King,
And share the deep thoughts of my mind.

As my passion becomes intense,
The urgency for me to write launches out at me!
I write about my past memories of experiences and my future dreams
      ahead;
I write my visions, goals, and destiny that are ahead.

I write.
Yes, my passion is to write!
So I rise up and write.
Life isn't over yet. It isn't even complete.
So yes, I continue to write.
I write about Him and me.
I write because of Him, for He is in me.

Dad's Power-Packed
Golden Nuggets
Geraldine Morgan

God can do more for you in five minutes, then you can do for
  yourself in a lifetime!

If you have the faith, God's got the power!

People don't plan to fail, they fail to plan!

You see my glory, but you don't know my story!

Excuses are the building blocks to failure!

Never jump into the water you're not qualified to swim in!

This year you shall become a God pleaser!

Why remain a slave when you are meant to be free?

Losers focus on what they are going through, while Champions focus
  on what they're going to!

When you let go of what is in your hand, God will let go of what is
  in his hand!

Pain is not an enemy, but is evidence of what exists!

Anything that does not change you, is unnecessary in your life!

When you discover your assignment, you discover your enemy!

You cannot sin and expect to win!

You cannot correct what you do not confront!

Every word either helps or hurts your faith!

One word is all you need. What are you doing with your word?

Somethings you need to forget in order to get what God has for you!

Every decision dictates a consequence!

You cannot build faith without love!

It takes time to become fruitful!

Climb out of your coffin and wake up!
You can make it because of the promise!
Work the word!
I am anointed to fight the devil!
My inheritance is locked up in pleasing God!
The Lord never gives you an assignment that He does not prepare
    you for!
Take care of God's assignment and God will take care of you!
Read the RED, and do what it says!
Submit to Destiny!
Speak life, make things happen!
Relationship with God must be built!
God did not hide things from you, but for you!
It's not so much what you hear, but what you believe!

MOMENTS, THOUGHTS, AND CONVERSATION WITH MY DAD

Geraldine Morgan

"Remember, it's the enemy's job to cut you off from your inheritance."

"You learn to know God by experience."

Over the years, I've learned there were three things my dad did not like. He didn't like lazy people, late people, and lying people.

Every morning, he spent time in prayer before he did anything else. He said to me, "You must develop a relationship with God that only comes from spending time in His presence."

I really didn't know what passion was until I watched my dad. He loved "SOULS"; that is how the tent revival was birthed out in the year 1972 in Jamaica, Queens, New York.

He reminded me quite often with the statement, "Give God a reason to let you live another day."

He was strong in his belief and the importance of studying the Word of God. He said, "It's important that you develop an appetite for the Word and the things of God."

He shared the importance of stewardship, accountability, and integrity constantly throughout his life.

God took a country boy from Bracey, Virginia and moved him to Queens, New York with a suitcase full of newspapers and one buffalo nickel. Then, God ordered his footsteps to the US Army where he became a sergeant. At the same time, God allowed him to cross paths with the love of his life, Margie. In addition, he opened up a luncheonette business and went into the construction business. And lastly, God allowed him to serve a pastor and church family faithfully for eighteen years, all in preparation for his ultimate calling as the senior pastor of the New Greater Bethel Ministries. This preparation lead to the tent revival on Frances Lewis Boulevard.

My dad was a man of faith and power. I find it amazing that God used an ordinary man to do extraordinary things. He touched thousands of lives by the radio and television and preached from multiple church pulpits, but his greatest passion was the Gospel Tent.

To Daddy, you left a legacy that will never be forgotten from generation to generation. Thank you for being my dad, my pastor, my mentor, and my friend.

ABOUT THE AUTHOR

"Passion is ageless. Tell your story and become a life-jacket for others."

Geraldine Morgan is a seasoned inspirational speaker, author, and mentor. She is happily married to Dr. Caswell Morgan. She is the mother of four children: Lora, Lance, Toby, and Dabari. She is also a devoted grandmother and great-grandmother. She has strong family values that are exhibited in her daily life.

In working diligently by the side of her father, the Late Apostle John H. Boyd Sr., founder of the New Greater Bethel Ministries, Geraldine has operated in her gifting of leadership and administration. Thru her experiences with her father, she learned to apply faith with demonstration, which is now exhibited in her daily walk with God. Her mother, the Late Mother Margie Boyd, inspired her to operate in the spirit of humility, with an excellent Spirit.

After thirty years of service in education administration for Bethel Christian Academy, Geraldine progressed to full-time ministry. She is presently on staff at the New Greater Bethel Bible Institute as an instructor on women's issues.

Geraldine is CEO and founder of Inspiration and Life LLC, Life Jacket Savers Inc., and the non-profit organization Helping Desperate Women Survive. She is also presently preparing for an upcoming podcast series and release of her new publications.

Geraldine has been awarded various citations of appreciation for her dedication to humanitarian services.

Geraldine is a designer's original. She represents the balance of dedication to her home, church, and outreach ministry. Her wisdom, knowledge, integrity, and steadfastness have enhanced her ability to become all God has designed for her life.

To contact Geraldine concerning speaking engagements, all requests may be sent to geraldinemorganap@gmail.com

For additional information concerning book orders and digital content, all requests and inquiries may be sent to geraldinelynnmorgan@gmail.com

CPSIA information can be obtained
at www.ICGtesting.com
Printed in the USA
LVHW020925210221
679521LV00005B/689